HANDICRAFTS OF BANGLADESH

Bangladesh has a rich and living tradition of craft and textiles that are closely linked to its vibrant cultural heritage. The crafts and textiles produced by its artisans reflect a heritage of thousands of years of history, folk music and literature. Firmly rooted in tradition the crafts are closely linked to the countries topography and climate, to its cultural mix and its age old customs.

Bangladesh has been the cradle of civilization, a center of cultural diffusion, since the dawn of history of mankind. It was the meeting ground of various peoples in different states of civilization, the most primitive as well as the most advanced. The cultural history of Bangladesh is one of the greatest and glorious heritages which every Bangladeshi is legitimately proud of. Each phase of the history of Bangladesh has its distinct characteristics and every race of people who came and settled here, left its individual racial, religions or cultural impacts in the form of temples, stupas, monasteries and mosques along with their associated objects.

Handicraft, also known as **craft work** or simply craft, is a type of work where useful and decorative devices are made completely by hand or using only simple tools. Usually the term is applied to traditional means of making goods. The individual artisanship of the items is a paramount criterion, such items often have cultural and/or religious significance. Items made by mass production or machines are not handicrafts.

Usually, what distinguishes the term **handicraft** from the frequently used category *arts and crafts* is a matter of intent: handicraft items are intended to be used, worn, etc, having a purpose beyond simple decoration. Handicrafts are generally considered more traditional work, created as a necessary part of daily life, while *arts and crafts* implies more of a hobby pursuit and a demonstration/perfection of a creative technique. In practical terms, the categories have a great deal of overlap.

Crafts of Bangladesh have a wide range. Some crafts are ethnic and traditional, some are new and modern. Some crafts are living while some others are dead. In any case, crafts heritage of Bangladesh is rich.

Crafts are made from a wide range of raw materials, available mostly locally. For example, from clay collected from around the potters' village, artisans make such ordinary consumables as cooking pots, utensils, storage containers, etc.; and from the same material they craft such exquisite things of beauty as images of gods and goddesses, dolls, flower vases, Lakshminsara, Sakherhari, jewellery, etc.

The raw materials used for making a wide range of crafts include metal (iron, gold, silver, copper, alloys), clay, reed (bamboo, cane, mutra, shoal, hogla, etc.), fibre (silk, cotton, wool, rayon, jute, coir, etc.), wood, leather, shell (conch, oyster, mother-of-pearl), animal waste (horn, bone, ivory, etc.) and other wastes derived from above and some such materials.

Irrespective of raw material used, levels and excellence of crafting skills have made some crafts ethnically renowned (eg. Manipuri, Chakma, and other tribal textiles), locationally branded (eg. Dhakai Jamdani, Rajshahi Silk, Shakari Bazar Conch-shell works, Sylhet Shitalpati, etc.), and crafting excellence (eg. Rajshahi Nakshikantha, Islampur Filigree work, Jessore Horn-Comb, Sonargaon Wooden-Doll, etc.).

Not enough praise can be sung about the ingenuity, skill and adaptability of the artisans who have kept their traditions alive over many generations. In almost all the small towns and villages in Bangladesh there are areas where artisans practice their crafts. Heriditary artisans have sustained their family trades through the centuries: the tantis /weavers, kumars /potters, kamars /brass smiths, sutradhar /wood carvers, subarnabaniks /gold smiths, malakars /shoal craftspersons and others have pursued their traditional occupations to produce crafts for daily use, for rituals and for decorative purposes.

In our Bangladesh we have improved on handicraft business. We are also exporting our handicrafts to foreign countries. We are being appreciated from those countries for our nice handicrafts. We can introduce our country with the other countries through this business. This type of business is helping to reduce our unemployment problem. Women are also working on handicraft. I feel that it is a good sign for Bangladesh. We have different handicraft businesses. Among them Nakshi Katha is a famous handicraft. It is not only famous in Bangladesh but also in other countries. A framed Naksi Katha increases the beauty of a room by hanging on a wall. It is used at home, office, shopping complex etc. In the rural area of Bangladesh"Nakshi Katha" is a common handicraft. It is an art of neglected village women. Sometimes, some fashionable women of rural area pass their leisure period by designing Nakshi Katha. Nakshi katha is a tradition of village. It takes tatters, cotton and needles to weave a Nakshi Katha. Women weave it with their creative skills. They make special designs with different pictures on it with the colorful cottons. It takes three or four months to make a nakshi katha for a woman. It is mainly used for bed sheet and blanket. The Bangladeshi people feel proud for this. Nakshi Katha can be used as a gift item for new couple, especially from bride family in the rural area.

Product where a lump of clay gradually took the shape of a finished pot with painted slips or a green bamboo went through splitting, bending and twisting producing a woven basket, are carefully documented. In the field of creativity, the artisan is not only concerned with the material and the technique, but carries a burden of the heritage to be continuously communicated to his clientele.

Bangladesh has a rich and living tradition of craft and textiles that are closely linked to its vibrant cultural heritage. The crafts and textiles produced by its artisans reflect a heritage of thousands of years of history, folk music and literature. Firmly rooted in tradition the crafts are closely linked to the countries topography and climate, to its cultural mix and its age old customs.

Not enough praise can be sung about the ingenuity, skill and adaptability of the artisans who have kept their traditions alive over many generations. In almost all the small towns and villages in Bangladesh there are areas where artisans practice their crafts. Heriditary artisans have sustained their family trades through the centuries: the tantis /weavers, kumars /potters, kamars /brass smiths, sutradhar /wood carvers, subarnabaniks /gold smiths, malakars /shoal craftspersons and others have pursued their traditional occupations to produce crafts for daily use, for rituals and for decorative purposes.

26/09/2005

Bangladeshi Handicraft: "Nakshi Katha"
In our Bangladesh we have improved on handicraft business. We are also exporting our handicrafts to foreign countries. We are being appreciated from those countries for our nice handicrafts. We can introduce our country with the other countries through this business. This type of business is helping to reduce our unemployment problem. Women are also working on handicraft. I feel that it is a good sign for Bangladesh. We have different handicraft businesses. Among them Nakshi Katha is a famous handicraft. It is not only famous in Bangladesh but also in other countries. A framed Naksi Katha increases the beauty of a room by hanging on a wall. It is used at home, office, shopping complex etc. In the rural area of Bangladesh"Nakshi Katha" is a common handicraft. It is an art of neglected village women. Sometimes, some fashionable women of rural area pass their leisure period by designing Nakshi Katha. Nakshi katha is a tradition of village. It takes tatters, cotton and needles to weave a Nakshi Katha. Women weave it with their creative skills. They make special designs with different pictures on it with the colorful cottons. It takes three or four months to make a nakshi katha for a woman. It is mainly used for bed sheet and blanket. The Bangladeshi people feel proud for this. Nakshi Katha can be used as a gift item for new couple, especially from bride family in the rural area.

The seller was showing Nakshi Katha in the fair

Now Nakshi Ktha is a famous and fashionable item of handicraft in the urban area. We can buy Nakshi Katha from different fair, shopping centre etc. In the fair most of the seller are women. The shopping centre Aarong is famous for Nakshi Katha design.

JAMDANI SAREES OF BENGAL

Jamdani is a vividly patterned, sheer cotton fabric, traditionally woven on a handloom by craftspeople and apprentices around Dhaka. Jamdani textiles combine intricacy of design with muted or vibrant colours, and the finished garments are highly breathable. Jamdani is a time-consuming and labour-intensive form of weaving because of the richness of its motifs, which are created directly on the loom using the discontinuous weft technique. Weaving is thriving today due to the fabric's popularity for making saris, the principal dress of Bengali women at home and abroad. The Jamdani sari is a symbol of identity, dignity and self-recognition and provides wearers with a sense of cultural identity and social Cohesion

Cohesion

Catagories of Hand Made Things
Bamboo Made:

<u>Excellent calendar made by bamboo.</u>
<u>You also can gift this item in any occasion.</u>

Excellent ornament box.
made by bamboo.
Very good to keep ornaments.
You also can gift this item in any occasion

Household products:

Made by Plam Tree leaf & rope.
This product can be use for keeping any things. It is also very good for room decoration.

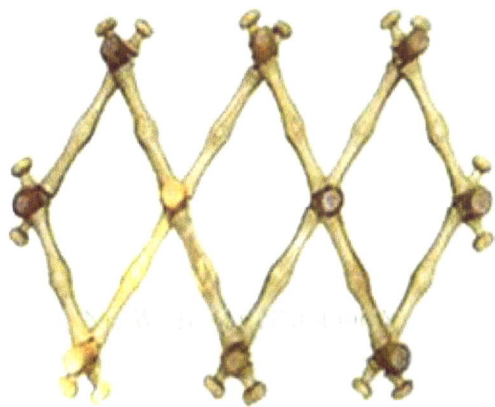

Made by Wood.
This product can be use as Cloth Hanger & Household products. It is also very good for room decoration.

Made by Wood. This product use as Lock-Key Holder.

Wall Mat and Calendar:

Excellent wall mat
You also can gift this item in any occasion.
This product use for Wall decoration. It is also very good for room decoration.
Made by jute

Printing (Rong Tuli) work
Size : 20"-4"
made by Wooden.
You can gift this item in any occasion.
This product use for Wall decoration. It is also very good for room decoration.

Nakshi Katha:

Size: Width = 5' , Height = 6'

Overall body katha hand stitch.
Manufacturer: Karupolly

This product can be use on winter season & Household product. It is also very good for room decoration.

NAKSHIKATHA OF BENGAL

Made by cable.
This product use as Showpiece and gift item in any occasion. It is very good for room decoration.

Excellent Clock
made by partex board & Plastic pipe.
You also can gift this item in any occasion.

Bangladeshi Handicrafts Success

Bangladesh handicrafts are always appiciated to the Global Market having some limitaion of marketing and communication gap bangladeshi handicrafts are not still remarkable above the possibility to increase domestic & global reach

Despite the fact that global exports of handicrafts took a big hit in the last 16-18 months, following the global slowdown, Gujarat based Self Employed Women?s Association (SEWA) has drawn expansion plans for its premium handicraft brand ?Hansiba?, which it had launched last year, along with aiming for a sales growth of 40 percent year-on-year.

Actually, those dark days, was the period when SEWA Trade Facilitation Centre (STFC) started diversifying by spreading its wings in to new overseas neighbouring markets like Pakistan, Sri Lanka, Nepal, Bangladesh and Afghanistan. Alongside it will also strengthen its presence in India by opening eight more stores in India, to raise its store count to 11.

Also, in the pipeline is an exclusive line of fabrics and apparels; ?Sabaah?, which will be exclusively retailed in the international markets. In a bid to reduce the impact of global slowdown, it will directly approach international retailers rather than through intermediates. In the previous fiscal, exports were down by 50 percent, which prompted STFC to take this decision. Fibre2Fashion spoke exclusively to Ms Reema Nanavaty, Director, Economic and Rural Development, SEWA, who spared her valuable time to speak to us and told about the future plans of Hansiba brand and the initiatives taken by SEWA.

We began this informative session by asking her to divulge the expansion plans of Hansiba, to which she said, ?STFC has traversed a significant distance along the path of building a successful business organization model, a company owned by the women artisans themselves as a sustainable business enterprise. STFC is now clear on the future journey. It needs to communicate the USP of ?Hand Embellishment? successfully through the brand 'Hansiba'.

?STFC has gained considerable experience in the retail market through both B2B and B2C businesses and feels that it is the right time to start focusing on marketing embellishments. STFC?s marketing focus is now to communicate STFC products, more so as ?Wearable Art?, rather than a garment. STFC?s proposed strategy will focus on the ethnic / ethno modern women?s apparels, home furnishings and gifts /accessories in the high end premium market, the mainstream fashion market and staple products market. STFC is entering into the high end premium market segment by co-branding with the labels and designers or design houses.

?The strategy is to market the embroideries and designs so as to ensure better remuneration to the artisan women. STFC plans to achieve 100% growth in business turnover in the next three years. In addition to this, there are initiatives like launching our crafts in neighboring countries like Afghanistan, Bangladesh, Nepal, Pakistan and Bhutan under the brand-name of SABAH. (SABAH is a noun in Urdu language, whose dictionary meaning is early morning breeze, which also denotes freshness.)

We than asked her about the market segment targeted by ?Hansiba? to which she said, ?We have three price segments; Premium collection, Special and Festive collection and a collection for Teenagers. In addition, we also have a collection of apparels, home furnishings, accessories, stationary & gift articles. The market segment targeted by Hansiba collection encompasses all the ranges; high-end premium market, the mainstream fashion market and the staple products market.?

Next we asked her what steps were taken by Sewa to reduce the impact of the slowdown on the handicraft sector, to which she replied by saying, ?With a view to demonstrate the strategy of inclusive growth and development and also as a response to the economic slowdown and the two major global crisis; financial crisis and climate crisis, Hansiba has come up with a new line of production and collection. SEWA Trade Facilitation Centre?s approach is to equip the women artisan shareholder in mitigating the two crises by accessing new markets and by building new skills.

To reduce the impact on the lives of its members, The STFC, a company of more than 15,000 women artisans and garment workers hasn?t resorted to subsidies and bailouts. Instead, it has forged a unique partnership between its shareholders – the rural women artisans and garment workers and international organizations such as the Alliance Fran?aise and international designers Graham Hollick and Corine Forget. Through this unique thread, local traditional skills connect to new global markets, safeguarding the lives and livelihood of the shareholders of STFC. This innovation is known as ?Ananta?, which is an informal workers journey to becoming secure, empowered artisan.

?Ananta, or the flamboyant stitch, has not only created the finest designs and embroideries for an international market, but has secured the lives of thousands of rural women artisans. Through Ananta the world will recognize our skills, which is providing its members with livelihood and security. We will not only host a fashion show highlighting the cause, but will also screen films, hold workshops, have dance performances and showcase the collection of garment and home furnishings made by the artisans of STFC, thus connecting local to global.

?Hansiba thus demonstrates a brand that is owned and managed by the women artisans themselves and for every purchase of Rs. 1.00 made by a consumer, Rs 0.65 goes directly in the hands of women artisans. Hansiba strives to market the skill base of the artisans which is the only source of income and livelihoods for the households. This in turn helps in maximizing earnings to the poor rural artisans, reduces migration and also improves education of their children?, she concluded by saying.

People have a distinctive sense of art. From the beginning of the civilisation they have created innumerable things as a blossom of this sense. They have done it from necessity or even unnecessarily because they are bound to do it. Some things they have preserved and made these a part of their living, their tradition. Some things they have abandoned as by anyway they feel these unnecessary. Handicrafts are by nature traditional. By using their primitive instruments, hands, people make these to use in their daily life. It is important to mention that most of the time handicrafts have an aesthetic view and artistic value. For this reason, historically the upper class of the society has a lust for these. In the timeline of history, patronised by the higher class people at different times, different pieces of handicrafts reached the peak of development and popularity. The handicraft products that are available in Bangladesh can be categorised as follows:

Of late, handicrafts have been exposed to commercialisation. Now, in Bangladesh, considering its potentiality in local and international markets, people involved in this sector claim for modernisation. New technologies and market competition always pressurise us to take steps to modernise this sector. Now, question is: how will we modernise this sector? According to some modernists, tradition is somehow a barrier to modernisation. But, without traditional touch, handicrafts will lose one of their unique features. Another fact is "All modernising society cannibalises their tradition, and in no modern society traditional artisans are survived." Japan, USA, European countries, all have done this. But in this case, China, India and Vietnam are different. China has preserved her cultural industries according to her own way by giving patronisation and policy-help. The modernisation concept is also slightly different there. The Chinese don't think being modernized, that is, being westernised. Their subjects, materials, designs etc, have been developed but not by abandoning tradition. "Jingdezhen in Jiangxi Province is a city famous for its 1,000-year-old handicraft industry, mainly porcelain making." The town, Lukang of Taiwan, is claimed to be the 'Mecca' of traditional handicrafts.

So, to modernise our handicrafts industry what model we will choose is a matter of some serious thought. However, our commerce minister has announced to formulate a national Handicraft Policy and we are passionately waiting for this. Because for modernisation or for any other development, policy support can act as a major contributor. Modernisation means creating well-trained artisan groups, adoption of technology in the value creation process, and establishing supporting institutions to a standard that will ensure competitive position of handicrafts in local and international markets. Creating well-trained artisan groups: "Craft works are involved with social relationships between producers and customers. The producers transfer social meaning to their products; customers decode the meaning and reinterpret it. Through this interaction, customers and producers share the same meanings, and the crafts are purchased". So, the people making handicrafts exhibit our social meanings derived from our values, cultural heritage, and tradition. To present the cultural heritage in the best way, the work of well-trained artisans is a good option. Now in Bangladesh, most handicrafts are produced, traded and exported by the giant non-government organisations (NGOs) and private enterprises. Among them, Karuponno Rangpur, Dhaka Trade, Kumudini, Aarong, Nipun crafts, Creation and Pioneers are exporting handicrafts to foreign countries. In these firms, there are professional designers with technical expertise. They design the products and skilled or semi-skilled people living in rural areas work at the dictation of the designers. In this case, creativity from the root level is automatically being discouraged. On the other hand, there are so many traditional artisan groups like potters, tatis, embroidery artisans, wooden craft artisans etc, living around the country who are supposed to be extinct because of lack of patronisation. The government here can choose these groups and can provide funding and proper training on technology implications, current trends and designs etc, under community-empowerment projects. Giving award and prize money on skills and expertise can stimulate this process of development. Arranging handicrafts fairs at national and international levels and encouraging the award-winner craftsmen to participate in these fairs can change the current situation. Adoption of technology: From production to sale to the customers, adoption of technology is a must to modernise the sector. Use of technology can reduce time and effort of the workers. By this way it can help to reduce cost and improve quality and make it competitive in the market. Re-sizing, shaping, designing, carding, and dyeing need technologies that the semi-skilled and unskilled workers are hardly able to use. Establishing and strengthening supporting institutions: Bangladesh Small and Cottage Industries Corporation (BSCIC) is responsible for promoting and caring the handicrafts industry. But unfortunately it has failed to carry out its responsibility due to corruption and mismanagement. So employing efficient and honest managers is a must to strengthen the BSCIC.

In line with this, establishing training centres at district levels, considering the specialisation of the locality, is necessary. For example, Tangail is specialised for "tater sari". So training on bringing versatility in making this kind of sari will be effective here. Combined research & development (R&D) centre: The government can establish a combined research and development (R&D) centre including different departments for different varieties of handicraft items. In this centre, experts will research the traditional design, styles and mode of production and develop new types of design, fashion and modes that will strengthen our competitive position in the international market. Students of fine arts and fashion graduates can work as interns here. Common Facility Centre: The Bangladesh Handicrafts Manufacturers and Exporters Association, popularly known as BanglaCraft has been demanding to establish a Common Facility Centre (CFC). CFC can enable the craftsmen to progress from individualised labour intensive process to a relatively easier production which can enhance their economic progress. The CFC can also be a platform for testing and establishing newer designs and prototypes as well. This is imperative so as to make the product more cost effective, marketable and self sustainable. A suitable common facility centre can greatly assist craft clusters to take advantage of modern facilities and move at par with the changing industrial and market scenario. This will help them achieve greater profitability along with necessary skill enhancement. As the market of our handicrafts is expanding in international arena, modernisation in this sector is so necessary to compete well. The government should come forward with the policy support and community empowerment projects. NGOs also should work for modernisation as they are already involved effectively with this sector. By their managerial improvement, new technology adoption private enterprises also can contribute to the modernisation of the handicrafts sector.

Preserve tradition of pottery from extinction

 From the very beginning of our Banglee culture, pottery has represented our identity and lifestyle. The artisans' works include making clay-pots, earthen ware, toys of clay and different idols of gods and goddesses have been the tradition of our culture. But it is now regrettable that in recent times, especially in the last decade **potters have been in distress**. Because of these unavoidable factors like clay, lack of capital, unsatisfactory selling of clay pots, lack of fuel wood for burning raw pots, their plight is in peril.

Earthenware and fashionable things of clay are being rapidly supplanted by aluminum, plastic, steel and other alternative materials. Even toys for children are being made with wood and cloth. Besides, so cold prestigious people never tend to buy earthenware thinking their image and status. But it is admitted everywhere that cooking pot of clay is more conducive to health than pot of silver or other materials. Cooking rice of clay-pots help to cure gastric problem. And pitchers keep water cool in hot days. Another cause for not selling clayware is its brittleness. Inspite of being more cheaper than other aluminum or plastic made pots, clay-pots are not being sold available. Thus potters have to survive with a negligible earning.

To observe the present condition of potters I visited Vaagandanga village in Faridpur, my home district on spot. A potter named Paras Chandra Pal told with rage, after liberation war many potter families had left the country away. The reason behind their leaving home allegedly are precarious future of pottery, oppression by neighbours as communal violence, political molestation & feeling of dire insecurity. He also informed that to bring money as a loan for capital from banks, they have to pay bribe to bank officials. NGOs often help them by providing loan with low interest. Potters are also concerned at the rising price of fuel wood and clay. Above all, their hard labour to pottery is not undeniable at all. Many of them grudgingly rush to adopt another occupations leveing pottery gradually.

Hence, government and connoisseur of pottery both should come forward to alleviate their poverty and evaluate their artistical work precisely. The commoner can also play a role merely considering the question of precisely. The commoner can also play a role merely considering the question of preservation of our Banglee tradition.

Shatranji: An old heritage

Shatranji, a variety of handloom carpet which is the heritage of Rangpur and the country, has had a chequered history. Once exported from Bangladesh to India, Pakistan and Sri Lanka it had earned acclaim for its extraordinary aesthetic appeal. Though Shatranji was produced profusely in the village of Nishbetganj (earlier named Parbotipur), technological advancement and colonial aggression led the craft to the verge of extinction. In a precarious situation, the weavers began to look for alternative sources of income.

Going back in time, the history of Rangpur has it that Shatranji of Nishbetganj was greatly popular in the Mughal period. In fact, it is believed that emperor Akbar used this Shatranji to adorn his palace in Delhi. Over the course of years, the cottage industries of Shatranji have been set up in Pakistan, Iran and India, using the techniques of the Nishbetganj. These countries have kept their industries running profitably and have also ventured into the export market. Another promoter of the craft is a Swedish organisation, which came to Nishbetganj with funds to revive the cottage industry. The organisation provided the weavers with money and purchased Shatranji in return to send to Sweden. However, a while later the organisation withdrew its support, leaving the weavers high and dry and spelling the end of the project. Fortunately, help was at hand. An entrepreneur Shafiqul Alam Selim came forward with a creative plan to re-establish the cottage industries of Shatranji at Nishbetganj.

Gradually, Shatranji earned renown with new designs and weaving techniques.Today there are over 300 Shatranji weavers. Shafiqul is highly optimistic about the future of this cottage industry. "I am an optimist and believe that talent and sincerity can lead to success. It is a measure of success that Shatranji has crossed the country border and is being exported to foreign countriesalbeit on a small scale.

Art of Rickshaw Painting

In Bangladesh, almost every square inch of the frame, hood and seat of these large tricycles is decorated. The decorations are traced around cardboard patterns, then cut from bright coloured plastic in bright pinks, yellow, blue, green, silver and gold, or painted on tinplate in the case of panels. Some artists earn their living by decorating rickshaws. Most images represent a dream world drawn from cinema, advertising and other popular media; they conjure up an urban fantasy of a peaceful and prosperous Bangladesh full of skyscrapers, brilliant colours, beautiful women and dashing heroes. Rural scenes are also very popular, such as waterfalls, snow-capped mountains, chickens, cows, ducks, palm trees, water lilies and boats sailing across rivers and lakes. Film stars are often vividly portrayed, as are scenes from the war that led to the country's independence in 1971.

The owners of rickshaws personalize their vehicles with elaborate paintings that incorporate floral and geometric motifs, animals as satire on human foibles or as themselves in combat, and religious themes, village landscapes and urban themes, and pictures of movie stars. Rickshaw art is an expression of the fondest desires in men's hearts-for wealth, sex, power, one's village home, religious blessings, and consumer goods

Joanna Kirkpatrick has photographed these vehicles for more than 20 years, cataloging styles and motifs. Her study becomes a window on Bangladesh culture and religion (Indiana University, USA, 2003). A movie banner artist touches up his masterpiece--the lush, enticing, and gigantic face of a beautiful woman, a film star, a heroine of movie nights in squalid theaters and the daydreams of ordinary men of the streets. Shadowed in blue, they penetrate the heart. She is the representative metaphor of this collection of ricksha art images, a popular medium which represents the heart's desires of ordinary men, as manifested in the objects of their gaze. This is genuinely popular art, similar to the hand-painted film billboards one sees across South Asia. Kirkpatrick carried out research between 1975 and 1998 in several districts of Bangladesh, though not, it should be pointed out, any other South Asian cities with cycle-rickshaws. She was able to differentiate types of rickshaw as well as distinct artistic styles,

Sadly, as she notes, the cycle rickshaw appears to be **losing out to motorized transport, despite the efforts of sustainable devlopment** agencies who correctly see the cycle rickshaw as a very efficient and appropriate mode of transport in the flatter areas of South Asia.

Generally speaking, in the eighties the elites of Bangladesh scorned ricksha art as vulgar while at the same time many fine artists of the country took it seriously as an expression of the taste and interests of the masses. I know this because I visited Dhaka Arts College and Chittagong Arts College and spoke with fine artists in those institutions. When I asked ricksha-wallas, ricksha artists, and sellers of ricksha decor who was the audience for this art, they all replied one way or another, "the ordinary people". One man even used the English word "ordinary", as in "ordinari lok".

What sort of art is ricksha art? From my outsider point of view, I consider it "peoples' art". It is not necessary to force it into a unitary category as it combines folkloric, movie, political and commercial imagery and techniques. It serves the expression of heart's desires of the man in the street for women, power, wealth, as well as for religious devotion. Ricksha art also serves prestige and economic functions for the people who make, use and enjoy it.

But let the ricksha artists have the last word: When I asked Alauddin in 1986 if he thought of ricksha art as fine art or as commercial, he said it was commercial art, which to him is art to be seen at a glance, not art to be studied and thought over, such as "fine art". That year I also visited an artist in Rajshahi (having first met him ten years earlier). The man is a prominent sign painter, ricksha artist, and decorative interior wall painter, to whom I put the same question. He told me a witty story about his puzzlement with modern art. He said he had been visiting the Rajshahi University campus to keep a business appointment with one of the professors. While there he noticed a painting hung up on a wall whose subject he could not decipher. It seemed merely a hodgepodge of painted swirls. He asked the professor to tell him what the painting represented and the professor replied, "A girl dancing". Trying to

understand, the sign painter asked, "But, how do you know this?" and the professor replied, "The artist told me!" (Joanna Kirkpatrick, 1997)

In Asia, there are all kinds of excessively decorated vehicles, and the rickshaw of Bangladesh is one of such kind. As can be imagined by its name, rickshaw is actually derived from the Japanese *jinrikisha*. Japan's jinrikisha, which was a leading item for export in the Meiji Period, was exported not just to Asia but as far as Africa, where its form changed to suit each locality. Even today, in Dhaka, capital of Bangladesh, the streets are filled with gorgeously ornamented rickshaws. While the folk paintings of Bengal District constitute their groundwork, they more directly refer to posters and calendars and, all over the rickshaw, they paint scenes from rural and urban lifestyles.

The Dhaka city had only 37 rickshaws in 1941 and 181 rickshaws in 1947. Before 1947, Dhaka was a district town, which had a population of 62,469 only according to 1951 census. But in 1998, the city's population grew over 8 million and the number of registered rickshaws in the city was 112,572. The number of rickshaws in all other cities of Bangladesh in that year was 274,265 and in all villages 91,040. Rickshaw and rickshaw vans (also a tricycle vehicle similar to rickshaw but with the difference that instead of passenger seats, these have a flat bed of wooden bars resting on the axle over the rear pair of wheels and they carry goods in small lots) are now fast replacing the traditional transports like horse carriages and bullock carts in the country.

It is a popular guess that the total number of rickshaws in the city is at least two and a half times that of the registered ones and accordingly, the city had at least 280,000 rickshaws in 2000. Estimates based on the figures that each rickshaw is operated by two pullers in morning and evening shifts and the average number of family members of a rickshaw puller is five, suggest that the rickshaws of Dhaka city alone is a source of income for nearly three million people.

Fifty percent of the value added in transport sector is being contributed by rickshaws and the mode of transport provides employment and living to people engaged not only as the pullers directly but also as its manufacturers of its mainframe, the body with seat and hoods and its spare parts. A great number of people depends for the living on the decoration of rickshaw body, artwork on it and rickshaw garages.

Art of Rickshaw Painting

In Bangladesh, almost every square inch of the frame, hood and seat of these large tricycles is decorated. The decorations are traced around cardboard patterns, then cut from bright coloured plastic in bright pinks, yellow, blue, green, silver and gold, or painted on tinplate in the case of panels.
Some artists earn their living by decorating rickshaws. Most images represent a dream world drawn from cinema, advertising and other

popular media; they conjure up an urban fantasy of a peaceful and prosperous Bangladesh full of skyscrapers, brilliant colours, beautiful women and dashing heroes. Rural scenes are also very popular, such as waterfalls, snow-capped mountains, chickens, cows, ducks, palm trees, water lilies and boats sailing across rivers and lakes. Film stars are often vividly portrayed, as are scenes from the war that led to the country's independence in 1971.

The owners of rickshaws personalize their vehicles with elaborate paintings that incorporate floral and geometric motifs, animals as satire on human foibles or as themselves in combat, and religious themes, village landscapes and urban themes, and pictures of movie stars. Rickshaw art is an expression of the fondest desires in men's hearts-for wealth, sex, power, one's village home, religious blessings, and consumer goods

Joanna Kirkpatrick has photographed these vehicles for more than 20 years, cataloging styles and motifs. Her study becomes a window on Bangladesh culture and religion (Indiana University, USA, 2003). A movie banner artist touches up his masterpiece--the lush, enticing, and gigantic face of a beautiful woman, a film star, a heroine of movie nights in squalid theaters and the daydreams of ordinary men of the streets. Shadowed in blue, they penetrate the heart. She is the representative metaphor of this collection of ricksha art images, a popular medium which represents the heart's desires of ordinary men, as manifested in the objects of their gaze. This is genuinely popular art, similar to the hand-painted film billboards one sees across South Asia. Kirkpatrick carried out research between 1975 and 1998 in several districts of Bangladesh, though not, it should be pointed out, any other South Asian cities with cycle-rickshaws. She was able to differentiate types of rickshaw as well as distinct artistic styles,

Sadly, as she notes, the cycle rickshaw appears to be **losing out to motorized transport, despite the efforts of sustainable devlopment** agencies who correctly see the cycle rickshaw as a very efficient and appropriate mode of transport in the flatter areas of South Asia.

Generally speaking, in the eighties the elites of Bangladesh scorned ricksha art as vulgar while at

the same time many fine artists of the country took it seriously as an expression of the taste and interests of the masses. I know this because I visited Dhaka Arts College and Chittagong Arts College and spoke with fine artists in those institutions. When I asked ricksha-wallas, ricksha artists, and sellers of ricksha decor who was the audience for this art, they all replied one way or another, "the ordinary people". One man even used the English word "ordinary", as in "ordinari lok".

What sort of art is ricksha art? From my outsider point of view, I consider it "peoples' art". It is not necessary to force it into a unitary category as it combines folkloric, movie, political and commercial imagery and techniques. It serves the expression of heart's desires of the man in the street for women, power, wealth, as well as for religious devotion. Ricksha art also serves prestige and economic functions for the people who make, use and enjoy it.

But let the ricksha artists have the last word: When I asked Alauddin in 1986 if he thought of ricksha art as fine art or as commercial, he said it was commercial art, which to him is art to be seen at a glance, not art to be studied and thought over, such as "fine art". That year I also visited an artist in Rajshahi (having first met him ten years earlier). The man is a prominent sign painter, ricksha artist, and decorative interior wall painter, to whom I put the same question. He told me a witty story about his puzzlement with modern art. He said he had been visiting the Rajshahi University campus to keep a business appointment with one of the professors. While there he noticed a painting hung up on a wall whose subject he could not decipher. It seemed merely a hodgepodge of painted swirls. He asked the professor to tell him what the painting represented and the professor replied, "A girl dancing". Trying to understand, the sign painter asked, "But, how do you know this?" and the professor replied, "The artist told me!" (Joanna Kirkpatrick, 1997)

In Asia, there are all kinds of excessively decorated vehicles, and the rickshaw of Bangladesh is one of such kind. As can be imagined by its name, rickshaw is actually derived from the Japanese *jinrikisha*. Japan's jinrikisha, which was a leading item for export in the Meiji Period, was exported not just to Asia but as far as Africa, where its form changed to suit each locality. Even today, in Dhaka, capital of Bangladesh, the streets are filled with gorgeously ornamented rickshaws. While the folk paintings of Bengal District constitute their groundwork, they more directly refer to posters and calendars and, all over the rickshaw, they paint scenes from rural and urban lifestyles.

The Dhaka city had only 37 rickshaws in 1941 and 181 rickshaws in 1947. Before 1947, Dhaka was a district town, which had a population of 62,469 only according to 1951 census. But in 1998, the city's population grew over 8 million and the number of registered rickshaws in the city was 112,572. The number of rickshaws in all other cities of Bangladesh in that year was 274,265 and in all villages 91,040. Rickshaw and rickshaw vans (also a tricycle vehicle similar to rickshaw but with the difference that instead of passenger seats, these have a flat bed of wooden bars resting on the axle over the rear pair of wheels and they carry goods in small lots) are now fast replacing the traditional transports like horse carriages and bullock carts in the country.

It is a popular guess that the total number of rickshaws in the city is at least two and a half times that of the registered ones and accordingly, the city had at least 280,000 rickshaws in 2000. Estimates based on the figures that each rickshaw is operated by two pullers in morning and evening shifts and the average number of family members of a rickshaw puller is five, suggest that the rickshaws of Dhaka city alone is a source of income for nearly three million people.

Fifty percent of the value added in transport sector is being contributed by rickshaws and the mode of transport provides employment and living to people engaged not only as the pullers directly but also as its manufacturers of its mainframe, the body with seat and hoods and its spare parts. A great number of people depends for the living on the decoration of rickshaw body, artwork on it and rickshaw garages.

- However, demands in the market, locally and globally, have in recent times led to innovation of new crafts, development in the mode of production and innovation in technology. Crafts production itself has gone beyond the barrier of caste and gender. Changes in demand, global competition and tariffs have also been reflected in the decline in some crafts and growth in others. These changes are worthy to be noticed so that traditional craft skills are not affected, leading to decline in production of specific crafts, or may be extinction

www.ingramcontent.com/pod-product-compliance
Lightning Source LLC
Chambersburg PA
CBHW060820290526
45792CB00005BB/1737

*9 7 8 1 5 0 0 8 5 2 9 5 5 *